ERIKA CARTER
Personal Imagery in Art Quilts

FIBER STUDIO PRESS

An Imprint of
That Patchwork Place

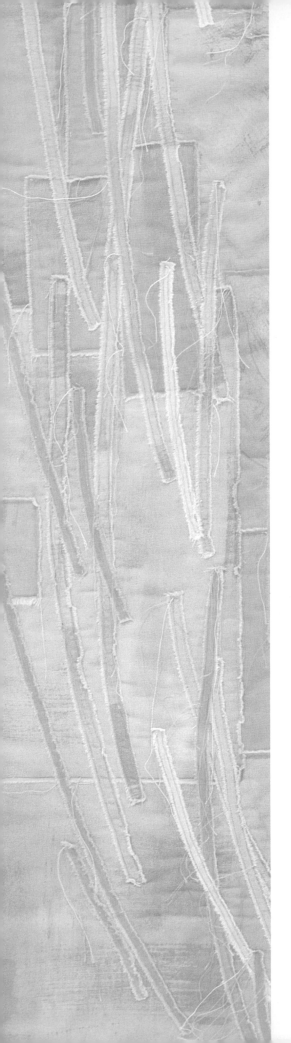

Credits

Editorial Director
Kerry I. Hoffman

Technical Editor
Laura M. Reinstatler

Managing Editor
Greg Sharp

Design Director
Judy Petry

Text and Cover Designer
Amy Shayne

Production Assistant
Shean Bemis

Copy Editor
Tina Cook

Proofreader
Melissa Riesland

Photographer (unless otherwise noted)
Brent Kane

FIBER
STUDIO
PRESS

That
Patchwork
Place®

MISSION STATEMENT

WE ARE DEDICATED TO PROVIDING
QUALITY PRODUCTS AND SERVICES
THAT INSPIRE CREATIVITY.
WE WORK TOGETHER TO ENRICH THE
LIVES WE TOUCH.

*That Patchwork Place is a financially
responsible ESOP company.*

The quotation on page 11 is reprinted by permission from Daniel Smith Inc.

Freedom's Cascade on page 47 is from the collection of the Museum of the American Quilter's Society, 215 Jefferson Street, Paducah, Kentucky 42002. Photograph by Richard Walker.

The photo on page 85 is by Carina Woolrich. Reprinted by permission from Quilt San Diego.

The photo on page 49 is by Susan Kahn. Reprinted by permission from Taunton Press.

Erika Carter
Personal Imagery in Art Quilts
© 1996 by Erika Carter
That Patchwork Place, Inc.
PO Box 118
Bothell, WA 98041-0118 USA

Printed in Hong Kong
01 00 99 98 97 96   6 5 4 3 2 1

Library of Congress
Cataloging-in-Publication Data

Carter, Erika,
    Erika Carter : personal imagery in art quilts.
        p. cm.
    ISBN 1-56477-147-4
    1. Carter, Erika, 1954– . 2. Quiltmakers—
United States—Biography. I. Title.
NK9198.C37A2 1996
746.46'092—dc20
[B]   96-1304
                                                  CIP

Dedication

For my mother, Mary E. Fillip, and my father, Hans J. Fillip

Acknowledgments

I am grateful for the love and support my husband, Howard, has offered over the years—from the early days of driving me to fabric stores and meetings, to more recently photographing my work. I am also fortunate to be blessed with two wonderful children, Andrea and Kevin, who are supportive of my artistic efforts.

I would like to thank: Nancy Crow for her generosity in writing the preface to this book. Since my earliest years as a quilt artist, Nancy has been an inspiration to me, as well as a mentor and friend.

Sharon Evans Yenter of In The Beginning Fabrics, for her support and generous contributions to our local quilt community, including her instrumental involvement with the Contemporary QuiltArt Association.

Rick Gottas of the American Art Company in Tacoma, Washington, for representing my work and for providing his gallery for a photo shoot.

The people and organizations who have shown support by purchasing my artwork, especially those who have later loaned me the purchased work for exhibition.

Laura M. Reinstatler, for encouraging me to write and publish this book with Fiber Studio Press.

Susan Ross, for her friendship, encouragement, and early reading of my manuscript.

Marty Bowne, Kathy Barker, Nancy Zee, and Leslie Leitch, for their supportive friendship.

And finally, a hearty thanks to all my talented friends from the Contemporary QuiltArt Association, for sharing their own stimulating and inspiring artwork over the years.

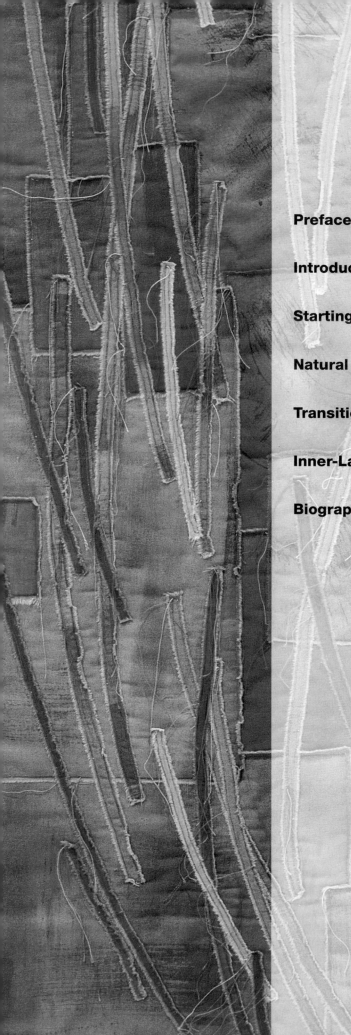

CONTENTS

PREFACE

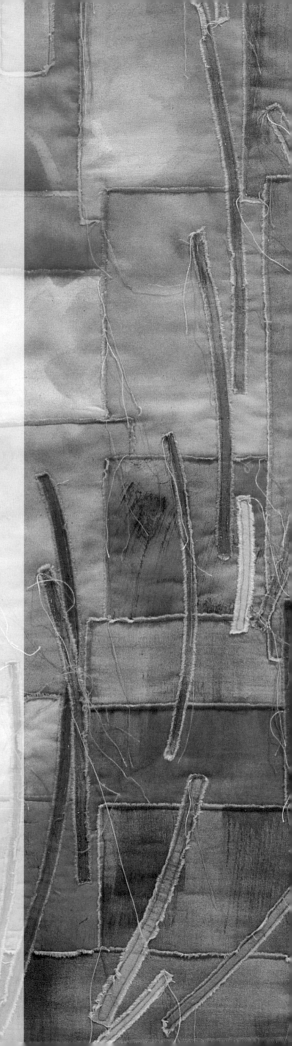

Intense. Questioning. Observing. Reflective. Soft-spoken. Emotional. Self-critical. Hard-working. Disciplined. Sensitive to her surroundings, to nature, to trees.

From the first day I met Erika, I knew instinctively that she would be adamant about developing her talent. She understood that one has to be disciplined and has to practice and keep practicing to get better. I liked her intelligence and her constant questioning. I saw how hard-working she was. She did not fall back on excuse-making.

Erika wanted to understand what it meant to be a serious artist and was willing to combine child rearing and studio work. Busy as she was, she also took on leadership roles supporting contemporary quiltmaking in the Seattle area.

In a comparatively short time, Erika has produced a large, strong body of work. It is clear that her vision has traveled a unique and connected path. Bravo!

Nancy Crow
August 8, 1995

INTRODUCTION

A Glance Back

Writing this book presented the intriguing prospect of reviewing the bumpy path behind me. This glance back has proved enlightening. I found the personal texture created by my having changed residences so often is perhaps the root of my attraction to fragmented imagery and ongoing attention to transition and change.

I was born in 1954 in Wiesbaden, Germany, and my earliest memories are snippets of traveling through Europe: creamy yellow buttercups; tall, lush grass; greedy pigeons stabbing stale bread crumbs; chocolate ice cream soiling my smocked dress; suspended bridges sewing together rocky mountain paths; noisy traffic in timeless cities; sturdy hotel beds

Few works of art are more satisfying to see installed than Erika Carter's fine-art quilts. These works add immediate warmth and vitality to any environment while adding a sculptural dimension that paintings simply can't match.

Rick Gottas
The American Art Company
Tacoma, Washington

with curious cylindrical pillows; escargot at a restaurant in France; and night trips in the car, watching the reflector poles pass in a sleepy rhythm.

My German-born father was in the U.S. Air Force, which ensured our family a move almost every three years. At the age of three-and-a-half, with a younger sister and a new-born brother, we moved to Hemel Hampstead, England. For a short time I was bilingual. Too soon, however, my early grasp of German slipped away and I began speaking English with a British accent. Memories of England include long strolls through public markets with stalls of iced fish, playtime on gleaming white beaches, green-pea soup served at nursery

school, unbearably itchy wool undershirts, and cold rooms without central heating.

When I was six, my family boarded a four-engine propeller plane, crossed the Atlantic, and I landed on American soil for the first time. In Rantoul, Illinois—the land of Piggily Wiggily grocery stores and the daily neighborhood Popsicle man—I lost all traces of a foreign accent. Our family grew by one as another sister was born.

From Illinois, we moved to what were then the wilds of Camarillo, California, where fields of lima beans and cabbages abounded. While there, I watched my beloved insect-collecting haunts become housing developments. Our family continued to grow as another brother was born.

I spent my fifth- and sixth-grade years in Glasgow, Montana, where I saw my first snowfall since traveling in Europe. The winters were bitter cold and the summers miserably hot, plagued by roving clouds of voracious mosquitoes.

By the time we returned to California, I was the oldest of six children (two sisters and three brothers—yes, another brother was born in Montana). We lived another two years in California, then packed and traveled to Wichita, Kansas, where we managed to plant shallow roots. After graduating from high school in 1972, I left my vagabond family to attend college in Boston.

While attending the University of Massachusetts, I lived in Belmont with my aunt and uncle, Ruth and Chuck Wells. They provided a nurturing environment during this period of my life. I graduated in 1976 with a Bachelor of Arts in German. Soon thereafter, I married my first husband, Robert Strauss, and we lived for five years in a tiny third-floor attic apartment in nearby Watertown. Tragically, Bob died in 1981 from injuries sustained in a car accident. In my effort to heal emotionally, I moved to the Seattle area. I now live in Bellevue, Washington, with my husband, Howard, and our two children, Andrea (born in 1983) and Kevin (born in 1986).

More Memories

I remember coming home from school to the combined aromas of home-baked bread and my mother's oil paints and turpentine. In the evening, after we children had gone to bed (at an outrageously early hour, I might add), Mom would continue to work on her art. Much of my color sense I learned by watching her paint. The layering and transparency of her watercolors left a deep impression.

Although she abhorred handwork, my mother learned to knit in England ("All English women knit," she wryly told me). One afternoon when I was eight or nine, she taught me how to knit and purl. That was when I discovered how much I love to work with my hands and make something new from raw materials.

It was my father who first amazed me with what a sewing machine could do. One evening when I was ten years old and needed an apron for a school activity, Dad decided to make one for me with the help of Mom's seldom-used Singer®. He had never used the machine before, and I will never forget watching with astonishment as an old sheet became an honest-to-goodness apron, complete with ties and gathers.

One year later, I taught myself to sew dolls' clothes by hand, and when old enough, I taught myself to sew on that same sewing machine. On a tight budget, with the desire to be more stylish, I began sewing most of my clothes and, later, most of my mother's and sisters' clothes. I loved tailoring and took on the challenge of making jackets and coats.

In college I reacquainted myself with knitting. During classes, between taking notes, I would knit. (My history professor called me Madame Defarge!) I made sweaters for family and friends—hardly anyone escaped my needles. I eventually taught myself needlepoint and experimented with my own designs.

Sadly, I never considered myself creative. The Halloween costumes my sister made (which held together for the single evening's excursion) were creative. My mother's oil paintings, watercolors, pastels, and pen-and-ink sketches were creative. Though my need to create was strong, I called what I did "practical."

Quilting, which I learned to do after the birth of my daughter, changed my way of thinking. Originally inspired by traditional quilt patterns, I quickly began to work on my own designs. At last I accepted the creative talent within me and began the arduous, rewarding journey of an artist on the path to self-discovery.

I believe each of us discovers something essential to our lives. For me, it is self-expression and self-discovery through art. I have found my driving force: the creative process. It permeates everything I do and affects how I feel about myself. No longer mired in the practical, I have discovered the essential.

The Work

The journey documented in this book begins with my earliest work. Each successive section addresses a level of development based on the prior work.

While this book is meant to serve as documentation of my development as an artist, I also hope it provides inspiration to others interested in pursuing their own creative imagery. Beginners will find support in knowing that inspired work usually doesn't "just happen." Art with integrity is a result of time, effort, and commitment.

Beginner or not, one can find encouragement in learning that the process is ongoing. It takes courage to go beyond one's comfort level, whether tackling the first original design or the hundredth.

There is value in viewing a single piece in the context of a body of work. Often the meaning of a piece is best revealed through an understanding of the earlier work. Though certain pieces stand out, it is the body of work that best signifies the dedication and commitment of the artist.

The following is one of my favorite quotes:

When we accept the making of art as a discipline and a lifelong venture, we then can relax and accept the fact that although we will never be perfect artists, we will, over time, be improved artists.

Dan Smith
Daniel Smith Inc.
A Catalog of Artists' Materials, July/August 1990

This statement supports my position that flexibility and acceptance are essential to the creative process. There is always more work to do; there are always more steps to take.

It's been an exciting journey thus far, complete with paths followed, paths ignored, free falls from paths abandoned, and thrills of accomplishment after reaching solid ground again. I know more twists and turns lie ahead, bringing dead ends as well as progress. My goal is to live an *essential* life. I now commit myself to this journey.

STARTING OUT
(1984–1989)

A passion for creating something of substance from raw materials led me to quilting. When I took my first quilt class in 1984, I knew that I was embarking on a creative journey. Already adept at many of the technical skills required to make quilts, I quickly moved past reproducing the traditional patterns that originally attracted me. I recognized the call to work creatively within the quilt medium.

So, the hard work began. Just as an artist in any medium must work diligently to find his or her voice, I knew I must make many quilts to understand what I wanted to say and how I wanted to say it. My first step was to become familiar with the basics. Classes, such as Mariner's Compass and Seminole piecing,

taught me traditional techniques and provided a structure for investigation. It didn't take long before I realized that, despite my inclination for order and neatness, I did not like precision work—even if I did design the blocks myself.

Beyond that, whatever was appealing became my guide. This was my opportunity to exercise self-direction. I studied the work of quilt artists I admired and, when possible, took classes from them. For example, I created *Untitled* in a Roberta Horton workshop that concentrated on using Japanese fabrics. Combining geometric motifs with nature images in yukata cloth and other commercial fabrics was intriguing and challenging. I also found it liberating to restrict

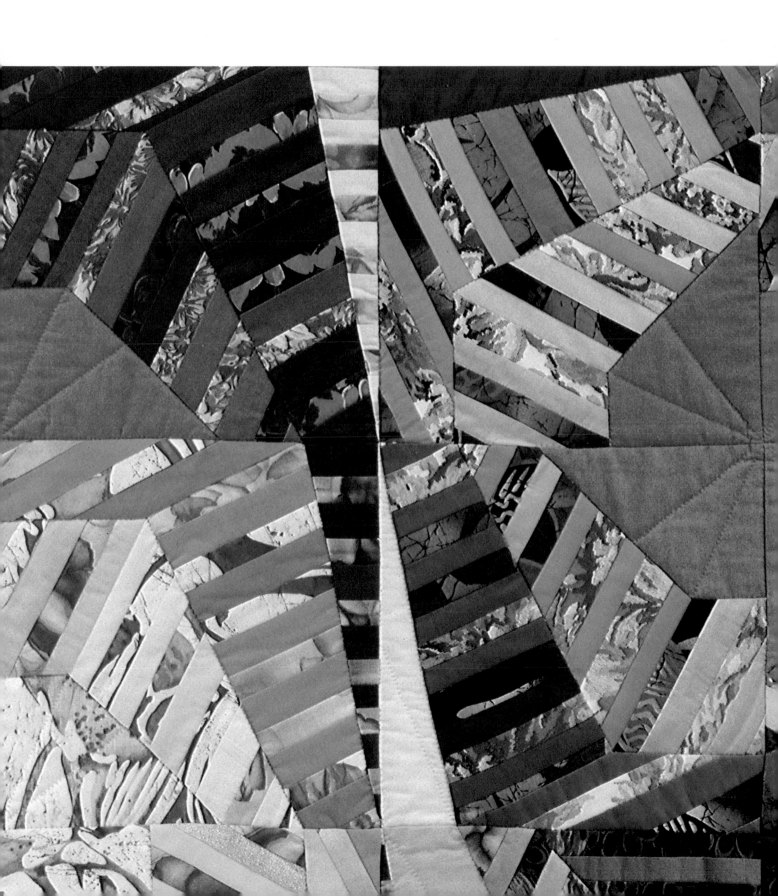

myself to a single shape—in this case, a long, slender triangle.

I developed *Horizon*, based on an original block that I flipped and rotated, using an exercise in Michael James's book *The Second Quiltmaker's Handbook: Creative Approaches*. Inspired by Joen Wolfrom's work, I created *Sails* as a gift for my newborn son, continuing my explorations with combining prints. One can easily detect Joen's influence in my use of the fabrics for the sky. My interest in nature imagery took me to a Nancy Halpern workshop, where I began *River Rock*.

Though these early influences were significant, Nancy Crow is the artist who made the greatest impression. A 1985 slide lecture was my first introduction to Nancy. Her words about

commitment, dedication, and integrity resonated deep in my soul, and continue to guide me today. She explained that producing art is hard work, and only by working diligently can one's art improve. Her words proved prophetic.

One of the more practical lessons Nancy shared was that quilt artists should develop their ideas by working in a series. My *Matrices* series was my first attempt to work this way.

After experimenting with pleats, folds, crumpled fabric, and beads, I began exploring the effect of yarns appliquéd to fabric. I worked in a series in which each successive quilt explored a new problem. (For example, I experimented with moving two color families from dark to light in *Hot Water*, and tried piecing curved strips in *Water Wind/Currents*.) My appreciation for the single repeated unit I encountered in Roberta Horton's workshop, combined with the influence of Joen Wolfrom's landscape work, contributed to my decision to use strips. By this time, I had begun to recognize my consistent focus on color and texture.

In my first workshop with her, Nancy Crow suggested I try using color as texture rather than relying on the hand-appliquéd, three-dimensional texture of the yarns. With that in mind, I began work on *Garden Play*. What a relief it was, not laboriously stitching all those yarns to strips! From that point on, my work had a different tone, and my use of patterned fabrics became more defined. I worked more quickly, focusing on design rather than three-dimensional texture.

In these first three years I produced more than forty quilts, some quite small, a few rather large. The more I worked, the more I felt like working; the more I produced, the more I learned; and the more I learned, the more I recognized how little I knew. The path ahead looked promising.

MY FIRST
©Erika Carter, 1984, 42" x 64"

I gave my first quilt to my first child, Andrea, on her first birthday. Begun when she was six months old, it took me six months to complete. Though I did not attempt to create a specific traditional pattern when I designed this quilt, I did design it to look like the traditional quilts I was familiar with: squares and triangles of calico.

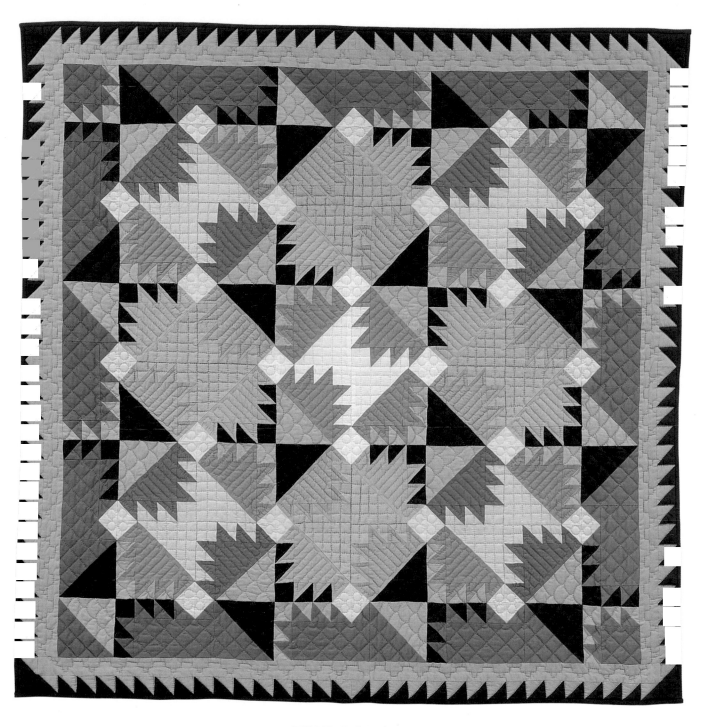

THE POND
©Erika Carter, 1985, 47½" x 48½"

I based this quilt on a traditional block.

UNTITLED
©Erika Carter, 1985, 24" x 63½"

I designed this quilt while attending a Roberta Horton workshop that focused on Japanese fabrics.

SUNSET DIAL
©Erika Carter, 1985, 50" x 51"

I designed the borders to complement the Mariner's Compass center medallion.

SAILS
©Erika Carter, 1986, 48" x 73"

Inspired by Joen Wolfrom's design style, I created this quilt as a gift for my newborn son, Kevin.

HORIZON
©Erika Carter, 1986, 89" x 89"

Bird images emerge in this composition, which is based on an original block. (Photo by Ken Wagner.)

RIVER ROCK
©Erika Carter, 1986, 39" x 52½"

I wanted this piece to inspire memories associated with souvenir rocks.
(Collection of Kurt Fillip. Photo by Ken Wagner.)

MOONLIGHT MATRICES
©Erika Carter, 1987, 41" x 34"

Suggestive of moonlight on snow, this piece was the third in a series based on an original repeat block depicting times of day. (Photo by Ken Wagner.)

HOT WATER
©Erika Carter, 1987, 47½" x 22"

Hot Water *is part of a series in which I explored texture by appliquéing yarns to fabric strips. This piece focuses on light and the interplay of two color families.*

WATER WIND/CURRENTS
©Erika Carter, 1987, 47" x 29"

Composed of curved strips, Water Wind/Currents *continued the series incorporating appliquéd yarns. The dark, rich blues at the bottom and the gradual change to light blues and greens at the top create the illusion of depth, while appliquéd bubbles suggest gentle currents. (Photo by Howard Carter.)*

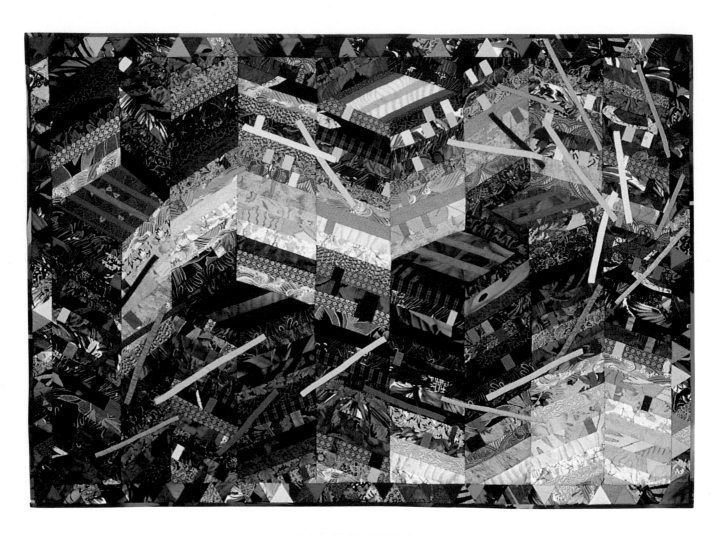

GARDEN PLAY
©Erika Carter, 1987, 41½" x 29"

I began this piece in a workshop with Nancy Crow. She suggested I consider using color as texture. This work represents fragmented growth and motion through abstracted nature imagery. (Private collection. Photo by Howard Carter.)

FABRICATION
©Erika Carter, 1987, 42½" x 61½

*Fabrication is the first piece in a series based on an original block. The dramatic color and composition
are indicative of the excitement and confidence I felt in the growth of my work.*

TRANSFORMATION
©Erika Carter, 1988, 46½" x 46½"

The second piece in a series based on an original block, Transformation suggests movement. Notice the increased clarity and definition that occur as the blocks emerge from the light. (Private collection. Photo by Howard Carter.)

COMMOTION
©Erika Carter, 1988, 63" x 52½"

*By modifying the block to resemble a flower and creating a naturalistic
background,* Commotion, *the third in a series based on an original block,
suggests the frenzy of color in a summer garden. (Collection of Nancy and Warren
Brakensiek. Photo by Howard Carter.)*

COLORIZATION
©Erika Carter, 1988, 52" x 40"

This work depicts the trend to colorize black-and-white films. The diagonal yellow and orange strips allude to color filmed in black and white. The diamond stage lights drop color bits onto snips of film. (Collection of Nancy and Warren Brakensiek. Photo by Howard Carter.)

NIGHT WIND
©Erika Carter, 1988, 38" x 53"

Returning to appliquéd yarns to suggest the grace of plants gently moving in a breeze, Night Wind *communicates the mystery of a garden at night. Do fairies really dance in the dark? (Private collection. Photo by Howard Carter.)*

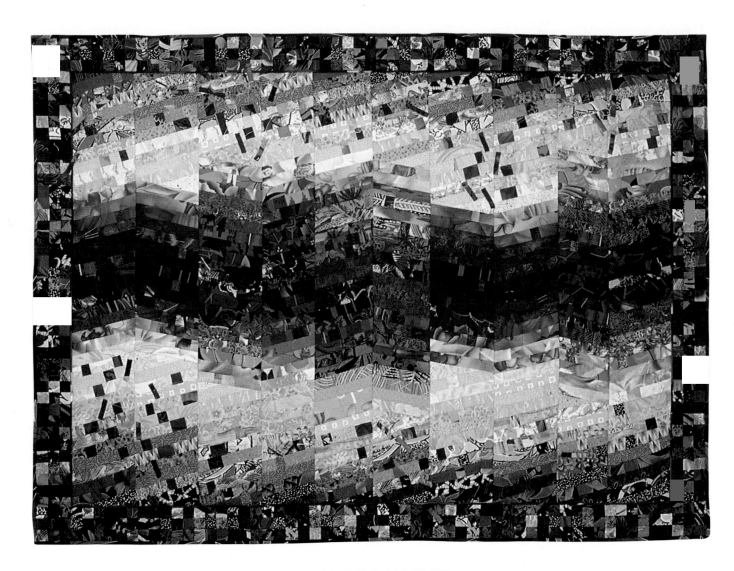

MUSING MAHLER
©Erika Carter, 1988, 54" x 41"

Musing Mahler *was inspired by a televised* Live at Lincoln Center *that featured work by Gustav Mahler. Tiny bits of fabric suggest notes exploding from instruments. (Collection of Dee Caskey. Photo by Howard Carter.)*

SHADES
©Erika Carter, 1989, 57" x 38½

After a winter's walk during which I noted the sharpness between sunshine and
shadow on snow, I created Shades *with soft, contrasting lines.*
(Private collection. Photo by Howard Carter.)

NATURAL INSPIRATIONS
(1989–1991)

The work from this period seemed to create itself. Already dedicated to working in the strip-composed method I had devised, I concentrated on communicating my love of nature (particularly for the Pacific Northwest landscape) and my concern for a healthy environment.

The view from my studio was my greatest source of inspiration. This view included the rhododendrons, azaleas, and firs in our yard and the various species of trees across the street. Beyond this were the reflective waters of Lake Washington, the homes of Mercer Island nestled in evergreens, and the spiked skyline of Seattle. On clear days, I could see the dramatic Olympic Mountains.

By appliquéing squares and rectangular strips of fabric to a background composed of strips, I created abstracted, fragmented images of trees, ferns, rocks, and water. Creating a landscape filled with realistic detail did not interest me; I wanted to create an *impression* of the environment. My designs took a spiral path, ranging from stylized imagery to abstracted representation, returning later to recognizable detail.

One can easily see that I was responsive to the Impressionistic works of Renoir, van Gogh, Monet, and Cézanne. I loved paintings that, on close examination, appeared as fragmented color and texture, only to become landscapes at a distance. At this time, I was so enamored with these artists' works that I found myself using painterly terms like "long strokes" and "short strokes" when referring to the fabric strips in my work.

This work was labor and time intensive. Although I machine-pieced the strip-composed backgrounds, I appliquéd and quilted by hand all additional imagery. The decision to hand quilt was an aesthetic one. I felt the broken, hand-stitched line complemented the fractured imagery.

Eventually, I chose to insert ultrathin piping made from a single print between the body and border of each of my works. This created another design element that held together the chaos of visual texture provided by the abundant, colorful prints. The thin, continuous line complemented the considerable piecing in the quilts.

As my work progressed, the fragmented imagery began to suggest time and memory metaphors to me. Each person's past is a textured, colorful path, remembered as fragments of a whole. These fragments sometimes blur, and at other times, vivid detail is present. It is difficult to hold a picture in one's mind for long without it changing. Rarely are the pictures sequentially connected.

Over time, while creating quilt after quilt, this fragmented structure became increasingly relevant to me and my life experiences.

My consistent efforts in producing and exhibiting artwork led to commissions, shows, awards, and occasionally, a fleeting self-confidence. At this point I had many ideas for new work and felt sure I would continue in this style. Unknown to me at the time I produced the piece, *Barricade* was the last in this period of work.

INTERTIDAL WILDERNESS
©Erika Carter, 1989, 57½" x 42"

The brilliant colors hint of life, mystery, and motion at the shore. I took the title of this work from a book by Anne Wertheim.
(Collection of Nancy and Warren Brakensiek. Photo by Howard Carter.)

SHORELINE
©Erika Carter, 1989, 63" x 42"

This piece was commissioned to resemble imagery used in Intertidal Wilderness *(opposite).*
(Private collection. Photo by Howard Carter.)

SUBMERGENCE
©Erika Carter, 1989, 71" x 53"

Submergence *suggests the attraction of the ocean and the desire to explore its mystery. The water's surface is within hand's reach, but the depths beckon. (Collection of the Museum of the American Quilter's Society. Photo by Howard Carter.)*

KALEIDOSCOPIC KELP
©Erika Carter, 1990, 40" x 59"

*Movement from dark to light in the background sets the stage for the gentle dance of underwater kelp.
(Private collection. Photo by Howard Carter.)*

SENTINEL
©Erika Carter, 1988, 38" x 72"

My first attempt at tree imagery, Sentinel *includes only a few rectangular strokes to suggest the tall trees of the Pacific Northwest. (Collection of Ruth A. Alvord. Photo by Howard Carter.)*

GUARDIANS
©Erika Carter, 1988, 47" x 55"

Inspiration for Guardians *came from autumn's reds, yellows, and browns, which appear as a blur when viewed from a moving car. (Collection of Sharon Evans Yenter.)*

AWAKENING
©Erika Carter, 1988, 41" x 81½"

Soft colors place Awakening *in the morning hours when light is gentle. Commissioned for a stairway, the imagery echoes views from neighboring windows. (Collection of Gayle Holeton.)*

BOURNE
©Erika Carter, 1989, 78" x 58"

"Bourne" means both boundary and goal. The meadow bordered by trees is the destination, offering an escape from midday heat. (Collection of Sally Reeve.)

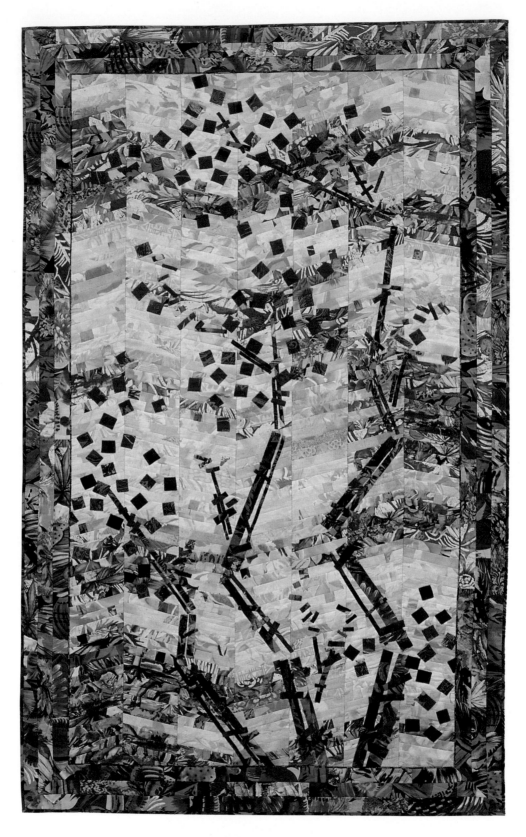

TENACITY

©Erika Carter, 1990, 45" x 73"

Strong, angular lines symbolize both age and the ability to weather life's challenges. (Collection of Jean and Al Koskie.)

FREEDOM'S CASCADE
©Erika Carter, 1990, 45" x 68"

Freedom's Cascade *was inspired by the fall of the Berlin Wall. The angular branches against the neutral background are reminiscent of the struggle for change, while the confetti-like flowers express the joy felt when change was accomplished. (Collection of the Museum of the American Quilter's Society. Photo by Richard Walker.)*

BACK COUNTRY
©Erika Carter, 1990, 70" x 70"

With a maze of colorful branches and trees rendered in an Impressionistic style, Back Country *conveys the chaos of woods in autumn. (Private collection. Photo by Howard Carter.)*

DEDICATION
©Erika Carter, 1990, 49½ x 63"

*Wild dogwoods become a metaphor for patience and dedication in this piece inspired by the view from my window.
(Collection of Hilary and Marvin Fletcher. Photo by Susan Kahn, courtesy of Taunton Press.)*

ELEVATION
©Erika Carter, 1990, 41½" x 32"

This work is a rendition of tall Pacific Northwest fir trees shrouded in distant gray.
(Collection of Kathy Barker.)

MAGIC MOMENTS
©Erika Carter, 1990, 50" x 43"

*Amoeba-like appliquéd images suggest dance and play.
(Collection of Nancy and Warren Brakensiek. Photo by Howard Carter.)*

BIRCHES
©Erika Carter, 1990, 55" x 35½"

A few simple, light fabric strips against a dark background suggest a grove of birch trees.
(Private collection. Photo by Howard Carter.)

WINTER WALK
©Erika Carter, 1991, 60" x 63"

Winter Walk *portrays Seattle's wet winter weather.*
(Collection of Omnitrade AB, Stockholm, Sweden. Photo by Howard Carter.)

ORIGINS
©Erika Carter, 1991, 59" x 55½"

Designed during the Gulf War, the intense colors in this work express the chaos of the time. Even so, the work addresses connectedness: the branches and roots of the tree become parts of the background, and the background, peeking through the strips that compose the tree trunk, becomes part of the tree. (Private collection. Photo by Ken Wagner.)

PACIFIC WOODLANDS
©Erika Carter, 1991, 59" x 75"

Pacific Northwest forest imagery was a natural choice for this wall hanging commissioned by Weyerhaeuser Real Estate Company. (Collection of Weyerhaeuser Real Estate Company, Tacoma, Washington. Photo by Ken Wagner.)

BEGINNINGS I
©Erika Carter, 1991, 66" x 54"

The diptych Beginnings I *and* Beginnings II, *commissioned by Swedish Hospital in Seattle, Washington, for their maternity floor, incorporates the spring imagery of evergreens, rhododendrons, ferns, and a flowering tree. (Collection of Swedish Hospital, Seattle, Washington. Photos by Howard Carter.)*

BEGINNINGS II
©Erika Carter, 1991, 66" x 54"

COTTONWOODS
©Erika Carter, 1991, 47" x 62½"

Through vivid color, Cottonwoods *conveys the vitality of the woods. (Private collection.)*

BARRICADE
©Erika Carter, 1991, 50" x 55"

Vertical and horizontal lines against a red-purple background create a barricade of tree limbs. The lines represent a forest's fierce strength and capacity for survival. (Photo by Ken Wagner.)

TRANSITIONAL WORK

(1991–1993)

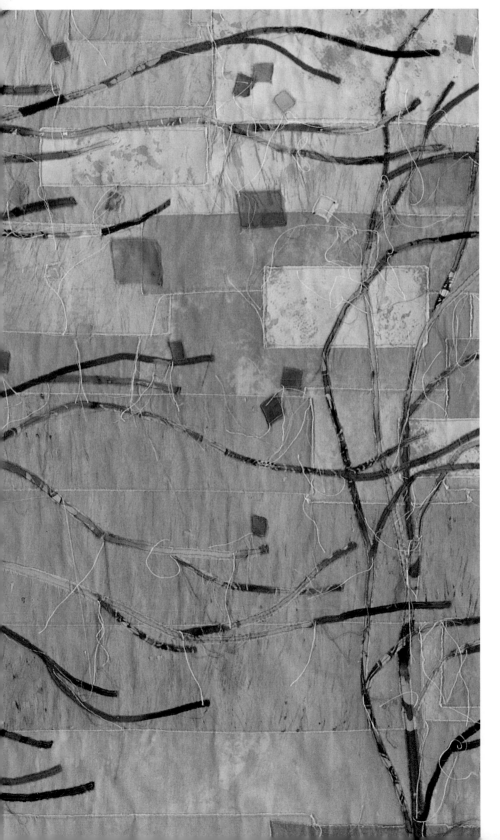

After years of producing fragmented, rigid trees built against a highly organized, pieced background, I found myself drawn to create more flexible images. These ncw images symbolized change and adaptability. "Management" and "balance" replaced "control" in my vocabulary for addressing concerns about the environment and my personal flexibility and growth.

This change in perspective began with another independent-study workshop with Nancy Crow in the fall of 1991. I made the painful decision to let go of the familiarity and success of my fragmented tree imagery and see what would develop. This significant personal challenge could be likened to blindfolding myself before crossing a busy street. Without sight, I'd have to trust my other senses and develop new skills.

Mindful of the stressful personal changes of the prior ten years, I was terrified of any further challenges. Though life changes are inevitable, I found myself fighting them. The significant difference with regard to my work, however, was that it was my choice to embrace change.

Of course, progress was not a direct path forward. After abandoning strip-composed backgrounds, I briefly returned to them, although in an altered form, in *Nurturing* and ... *For the Forest*. Much of this work reflected my "blurred vision," insecurity, and the tightrope

tension I felt because I didn't know in what direction I was moving. At the same time, however, I experienced a new sense of freedom.

I took numerous classes: machine embroidery with Barbara Lee Smith, hand embroidery and use of transfer dyes with Jan Beaney, painting with pigment with Richard Daehnert, and painting with dye with Ann Johnston.

A pivotal point was a workshop with David Walker. He created an environment in which I learned to look within myself for inspiration. Thereafter, my work revealed an increased awareness of and involvement with my inner self. Through my new work, I began to experience personal growth.

This body of work is a visual diary. My artwork's evolution can be traced by the change in my use of rectangles and squares. The angular trees from my earlier style (e.g., *Tenacity* and *Barricade*) evolved into flexible, healing grass images (e.g., *Ripple*). Made of torn fabrics, metaphors for the acceptance of change, the angular trees evolved into flowing, graceful images (e.g., *Arise*).

Journal writing became an important creative tool. Combining words and sketches, I fleshed out my ideas, recorded fleeting inspirations before they could be lost, and entered into a dialogue with my work to discover new possibilities and deeper layers of understanding. My journal became a place to expose my rough edges and not worry about mistakes.

Using pens, pencils, gouache, and pastels, I informally explored my ideas and stumbled upon a composition or thought that might not have surfaced so quickly using other media. However, I always felt most involved when working directly with fiber.

Though based on a desire to work more freely and to address flexibility, my decision to use torn fabric also led to an increased awareness of fabric's structure. The repeated process of tearing fabric provided a broadened sensitivity to structure as subject matter, and greatly influenced the future direction of my work.

SHATTERED
©Erika Carter, 1991, 40" x 30½"

Like shattered marble, this work suggests the chaos, challenge, and discomfort of change.
(Collection of Joanne Schwartz. Photo by Howard Carter.)

... FOR THE FOREST
©Erika Carter, 1991, 32½" x 49"

The title is a play on the adage, "you can't see the forest for the trees." When faced with the enormity of some situations, it is sometimes difficult to see the individual parts and begin the process of assimilation. (Collection of Ed and Rasa Knudson. Photo by Howard Carter.)

SUBTLE-TREES
©Erika Carter, 1991, 56" x 46"

For Subtle-Trees, *I intentionally played with the tree images against the background. Now you see them, now you don't. Clarity of vision is not always attainable. (Collection of Janet Haynes. Photo by Howard Carter.)*

TRANSITION
©Erika Carter, 1992, 60" x 86"

This work addresses the courage needed to take responsible action to encourage change. The door is composed of bright, inviting colors. Three keys at the door's base symbolize the need for action. One must pick up the right key and unlock the door to go through it. (Collection of Nancy and Warren Brakensiek. Photo by Ken Wagner.)

NURTURING
©Erika Carter, 1992, 51" x 51"

*After creating many quilts with tree imagery, I realized how much I identified with these images. Putting
stylized hands at the end of the tree's branches enhances this identification and creates a metaphor for nurturing
and motherhood. I used Bird Ross's manual zigzag technique to appliqué the tree's square leaves.
(Collection of George and K.J. Casady. Photo by Ken Wagner.)*

PLAINS
©Erika Carter, 1992, 36" x 26½"

This is the second in my journey series inspired by a vivid daydream. Plains depicts a desert that must be traversed, a metaphor for the desire for personal growth. (Private collection. Photo by Howard Carter.)

HANDLE WITH CARE
©Erika Carter, 1992, 32½" x 35"

The teapot is based on one I bought in Stockholm, Sweden. The teapot, a fragile item used with friends and family, becomes a metaphor for our relationships and how they, too, need to be "handled with care." (Private collection.)

BALANCING ACT
©Erika Carter, 1992, 60" x 66"

Trees becomes a metaphor for the difficulty of balancing many roles, such as wife, mother, artist, and teacher.
(Photo by Ken Wagner.)

SUNFLOWERS
©Erika Carter, 1992, 45½" x 74"

Sunflowers *is part of a series that uses grasses as a metaphor for flexibility.*
The childlike spiral flowers allude to life symbols.

BOUNDARIES
©Erika Carter, 1992, 61½" x 36"

Water surrounded by grasses is another metaphor for flexibility.

RIPPLE
©Erika Carter, 1993, 62" x 49"

Ripple *continues my series using grass imagery. Curved lines and brushstrokes of*
pigment on the background fabrics strengthen the movement and drama.
(Collection of Jim and Robbie Legus. Photo by Howard Carter.)

CENTERED
©Erika Carter, 1993, 44½" x 64"

Grass growing from defined areas refer to health and comfort. (Collection of Sally Reeve.)

ARISE
©Erika Carter, 1993, 44" x 68"

This piece's imagery began as grass and emerged as a tree, much to my delight. Unlike my earlier, more rigid tree images, curved lines speak of flexibility. (Collection of Nancy E. Powell. Photo by Howard Carter.)

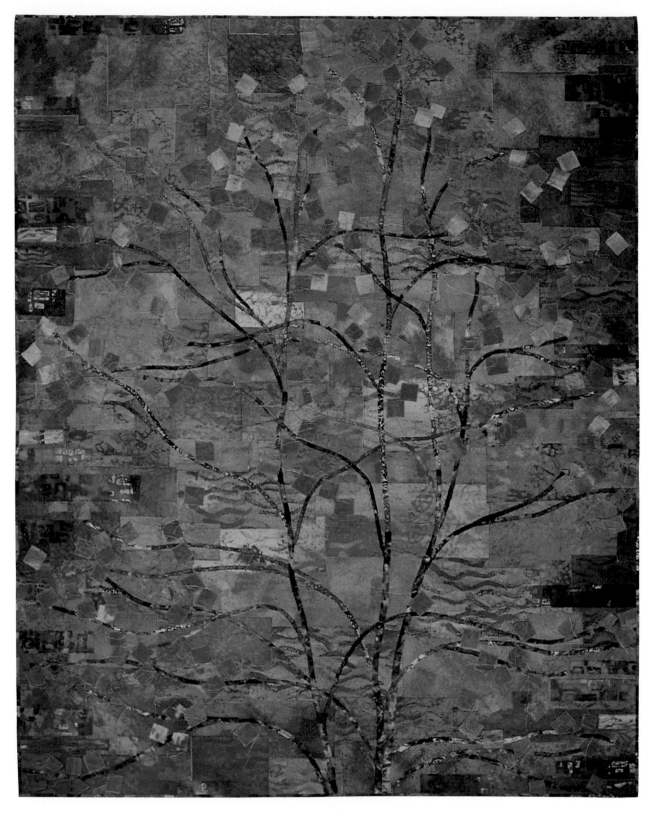

ARISEN
©Erika Carter, 1993, 50" x 63"

Inspired by Arise *(page 76), this piece also addresses the positive nature of flexibility.*
(Private collection. Photo by Howard Carter.)

UNFOLDING
©Erika Carter, 1993, 54½" x 71"

*A flowering tree is a metaphor for the rewards of accepting and meeting a
challenge. The spiral "flowers" are life signs, and the machine-embroidered hands
refer to the human presence in my work.*

ASSENT
©Erika Carter, 1993, 67" x 44½"

This work is about accepting change. Change may be a release, an unloading of extra weight to make way for growth and new ideas. While Assent uses autumn as a metaphor, the spring green in the background suggests the promise of tomorrow. (Collection of Andrea and Van Vanosdoll.)

INNER-LANDSCAPE WORK
(1993 TO PRESENT)

In 1993, while attending an independent-study workshop with Linda MacDonald at the Quilt Surface Design Symposium, I found myself working on a self-determined problem that called for an abstract solution. I wanted to address sensitivity, that delicate slice of personality that can undermine as easily as it can strengthen.

Resolving my abstract composition was far more difficult than I had expected. This difficulty caught me off guard and puzzled me. That's when I realized that my work was again becoming too predictable, that I was relying too much on a landscape format to express my ideas.

For days I worked at my abstract composition, arranging and rearranging elements, never feeling that the results were successful. The piece eventually evolved into a work about process, creativity, and the tentative nature of learning. I recorded this struggle in my journal, hoping that acknowledging the problem would lead to an answer. At home after the workshop, I decided to be patient and allow the dilemma to resolve itself in its own time.

I returned to landscape compositions for a few months. *Assent*, which uses autumnal tree imagery as a metaphor for accepting change, was inspired by this decision to trust myself. The trees, bent gracefully in the wind, do not break, but simply let go of their burden to make way for new growth.

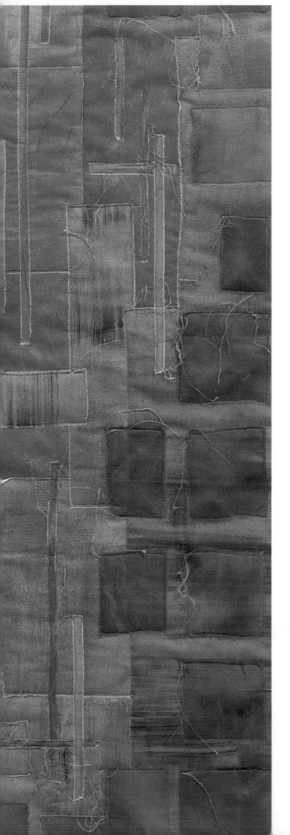

Indeed, about three months after the crisis, without consciously trying to address the issue of abstract composition, I created *Parameters*. This piece bridges abstract and landscape imagery. The grasses symbolize the success and growth one can experience when working within defined parameters; the silk organza squares in the right and left margins represent those parameters. My patience paid off, and since making this crucial piece, all my work has relied on abstract composition to communicate ideas.

Personal, internal landscapes are organic. They live, change, and grow. Some aspects wither and die. My original interest in the organic—the external landscape or environment—led to my expression of the internal landscape. I developed a new vocabulary to relate the organic to the personal landscape. I used columns, windows, and boxes as metaphors for issues such as success, chaos, depression, and growth. These metaphors became tools with which to articulate the challenges faced in day-to-day life.

My work habits began to change. In the past, I would finish a piece and almost immediately begin the next. Rarely was I without a quilt in progress. Gradually, I found I could no longer produce one piece right after another. I needed to allow breaks, periods when my mind could lay fallow while new ideas germinated. This down time lasted anywhere from one week to a month or more. The longer it lasted, the tougher it became to remain patient, and I would entertain thoughts of inadequacy and self-doubt. Then new ideas would emerge and, relieved, I could work swiftly and steadily.

My work took greater concentration than it had in the past, especially when I began a new piece. Interruptions could be devastating, causing a lack of focus. Once started again, however, I gladly gave myself over to the highs and lows of the psychologically bumpy process of creating a new work.

Periods when I wasn't working on a piece became time to read and study other artists' work. Moving away from the Impressionists, I found myself attracted to artists such as Mark Rothko and Richard Diebenkorn, for their evocative use of space; Hundertwasser, for his use of line and color; Ritzi Jacobi, for her rich, textured fiber structures; Agnes Martin, for her minimal color and repetitive, meditative shapes; Susan Rothenberg, for her expressive brush strokes; and Magdalena Abacanowitz, for her powerful, monumental sculptural work.

I belong to a subgroup of the Contemporary QuiltArt Association that is an arena for studying art on a theoretical and critical basis. As my acceptance and appreciation for more kinds of art developed, I learned the role context plays in evaluating works of art. The same criteria need not always apply. This prompted me to ask, What I am doing now? In what context is it being done? and Why am I doing it? Informed by that moment's "correct" answers, I'd move forward.

What lies ahead? Of course, no one knows for sure. I have always been a traveler, and through my art I have learned a new way to travel. At the beginning of my quiltmaking journey, I didn't know what I wanted to say, nor did I have the tools to begin discussion. After more than twelve years on this path of discovery, I've developed a personal language for discussing the human condition through my work. I've replaced a search for self-expression with a search for self-knowledge. Using my life experiences as inspiration, I attempt to address issues common to us all, adding to the continuing dialogue of what it is to be human.

PARAMETERS
©Erika Carter, 1993, 65" x 45"

*This is the first in a series addressing boundaries and definitions. The grasses are
a metaphor for the success and growth one can experience when working within
defined limits. (Private collection. Photo by Strode Photographers.)*

PARAMETERS: CHAOS
©Erika Carter, 1993, 67½" x 45"

The myriad squares and thin rectangles to the right and left of the center allude to power, creativity, and the occasional pattern inherent in chaos. It is human nature to attempt to create order out of chaos. The machine-stitched hands amid the structured center squares further depict the human element. (Private collection. Photo by Carina Woolrich, courtesy of Quilt San Diego.)

PARAMETERS: BREAKDOWN
©Erika Carter, 1993, 68" x 45"

This piece is about redefining the parameters within which one strives to succeed and grow. Here the parameters have been in place too long. It is time to break down old barriers and attempt to tap new energy, represented by the yellow margins. (Collection of Katherine Freeman.)

SHARED PARAMETERS
©Erika Carter, 1993, 38½" x 43"

Shared Parameters *is about kindred spirits. It addresses, in abstract terms, the overlapping of personal traits that occurs in friendships and marriage, or simply the sense of connection one person might feel toward another. (Photo by Howard Carter.)*

ENCLOSURE
©Erika Carter, 1994, 65½" x 44½"

Originally inspired by boxed-in feelings created by the holidays, Enclosure *evolved into a work addressing inner self versus the well-cared-for image we project to others. It is an image that both protects and separates what may be common to all. (Private collection. Photo by Howard Carter.)*

PARAMETERS: WINDOW
©Erika Carter, 1994, 58" x 58"

*Within the large wall space is a window: a metaphor for change, an entrance or
exit, a bridge between inside and outside, a threshold, and a call for action. The
thin fabric strips, composed to imitate weaving, suggest organic origins.*

PARAMETERS: CHOICES
©Erika Carter, 1994, 58½" x 56½"

Parameters: Choices *is about creative thinking. Numerous windows emerging
from the background suggest the brainstorming that develops new ideas.
The spring green of the background refers to the positive nature, the promise,
of active thought. The thin, intersecting torn strips and machine quilting allude
to the work's organic beginnings—the weaving of fabric, as well as to
issues of personal structure.*

COLUMNS
©Erika Carter, 1994, 47" x 61½"

This is the first in a series using architectural columns as a metaphor for personal, internal structural support units.

COLUMNS II
©Erika Carter, 1994, 48" x 59"

Dark columns, composed of layered cotton and silk organza rectangles, dominate the composition with both their color and dimension, emanating power and confidence. The yellow-green background pushes forward dramatically, creating the illusion of secondary columns.

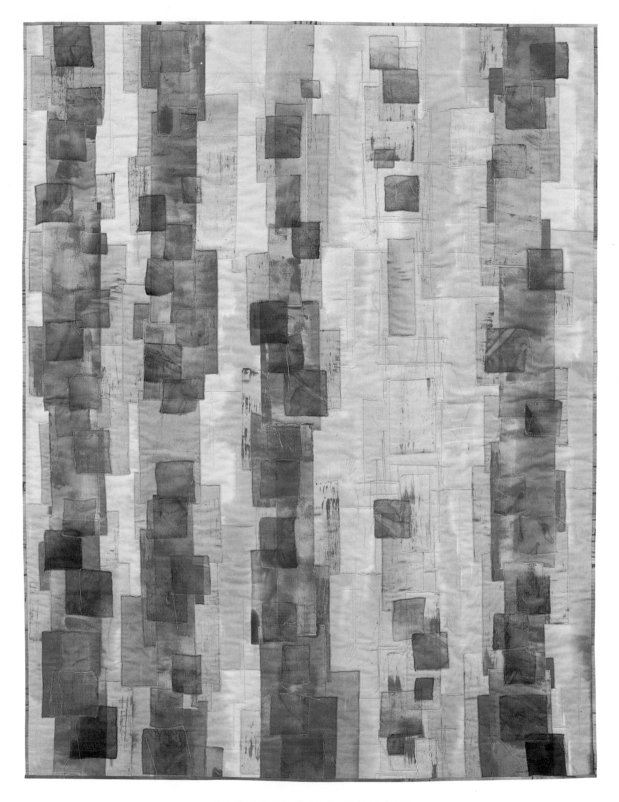

COLUMNS III: REPAIR
©Erika Carter, 1994, 45" x 59½"

These columns are more slender and fragile than in earlier works. One of the support units is under repair, addressing the issues of self-confidence, work, and recovery. Tiny hands among the machine-stitched lines indicate an internal process.

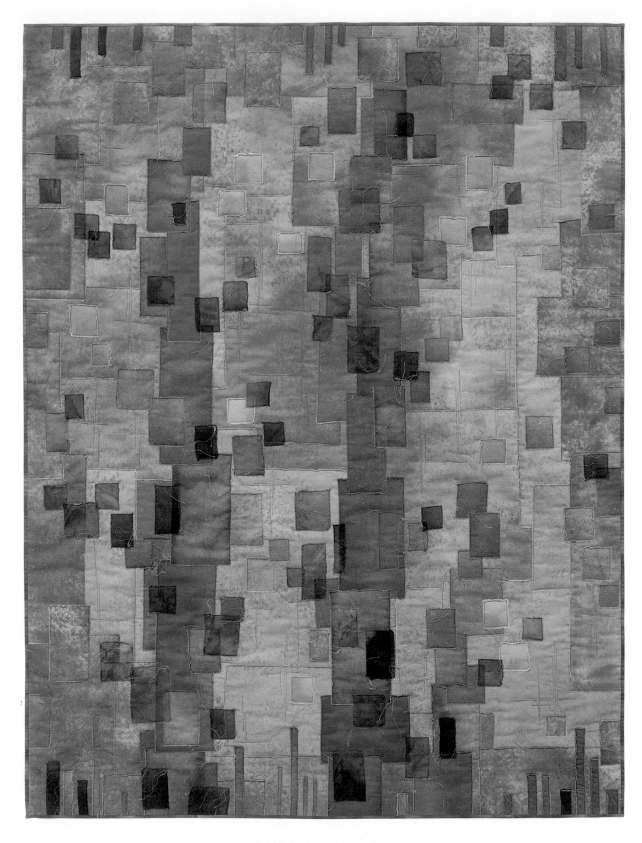

REMINISCENT
©Erika Carter, 1994, 44½" x 60"

Continuing my Columns series, the columns in this piece allude to the familiar trees of my earlier work.

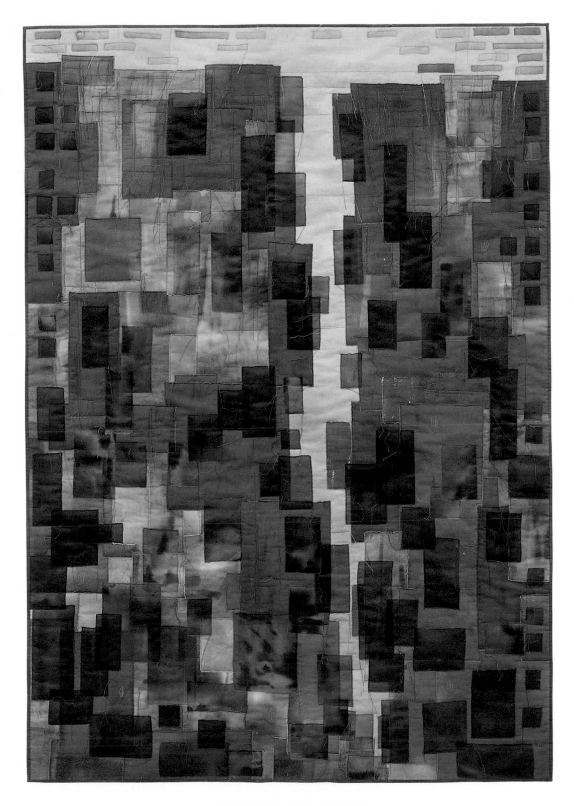

CONFINEMENT
©Erika Carter, 1994, 45" x 65"

Rectangular strips on the elevated horizon contribute to the illusion of being forced down into the crevice, committed to the dark journey. A multitude of untrimmed threads near the horizon suggest the organic nature of this journey. The small squares on the left and right margins contribute to the sense of confinement, the lack of obvious options.

CONNECTIONS (BRIDGES/FENCES)
©Erika Carter, 1994, 46" x 57½"

Connections (Bridges/Fences) *is a metaphor for communication. Sometimes communication works, bridging the gap between people; and sometimes it breaks down, acting as a fence or barrier.*

TRANSITION II
©Erika Carter, 1994, 34" x 47½"

This work addresses change. Supported within the depths of the flexible grasses, a door emerges. The warm yellows represent inner light. (Collection of the American Craft Museum, New York, New York. Photo by Howard Carter.)

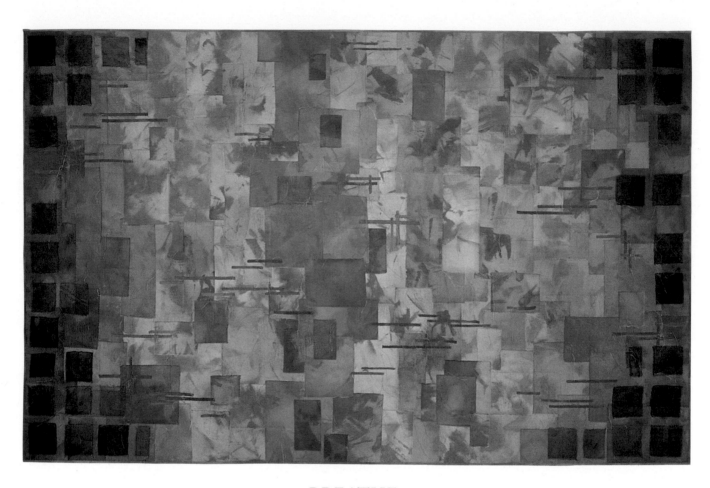

BREATHE
©Erika Carter, 1994, 71" x 46"

Breathing can be seen as a metaphor for communication. When one breathes, each breath is an exchange, inhale / exhale, a give and take. To be healthy, cooperation must exist among all parts. In Breathe, color suggests both the structure and movement of a breath. Within the light areas to the left and right of the green center, brush strokes resemble the turbulence of air movement. The thin horizontal fabric lines and quilted lines carry perimeter and center colors back and forth across the quilt. (Photo by Howard Carter.)

PARAMETERS: COST
©Erika Carter, 1994, 46" x 69"

This is about depression, when the inner light seems to be going out, turning ashen, and one is surrounded by a blanket of gray stillness. It is a time one cannot ignore, a time of rest. Though it seems hard to imagine, important inner restructuring may be taking place at a different, as yet hidden, level, suggested here by the occasional hand-quilted lines.

PARAMETERS: SHIFT
©Erika Carter, 1994, 67" x 45"

Parameters: Shift *is about inner change, the profound instability one feels when one's boundaries seem to be in continuous flux. Both hot and cool colors are present in the work, symbolizing the highs and lows of dealing with change.*

PARAMETERS: CHRYSALIS
©Erika Carter, 1995, 46" x 70"

This piece continues my gray series about the challenge of change. Horizontal lines and fabric strips on the sides suggest the peeling back of layers—or fibers—exposing the metamorphosis taking place within. The yellow center is brighter and more promising than in Parameters: Cost. *The* X*s in the central area, both painted and stitched with thread, hint at structuring the new body. I used the* X *because it connotes both "X marks the spot" and "X means not here."*

SUPPORT I
©Erika Carter, 1995, 46" x 49"

A vertical line of silk organza rectangles, the structural backbone of the quilt, symbolizes support. The thin, mostly horizontal strips become additional support elements.

SUPPORT II
©Erika Carter, 1995, 46" x 48½"

*The suggestion of "body" is enhanced through built-up horizontal areas of color,
reinforcing the quilt's spine / support metaphor.*

SUPPORT III: PAST
©Erika Carter, 1995, 46" x 50"

With so much of my work about change, I began to consider how some aspects of who we are never change. Inspired by a book on cave paintings, I used grays and the texture of rock as the backdrop for the spiritlike backbone of silk organza squares. Reminiscent of X-rays, they suggest the constant presence of the past.

SUPPORT V
©Erika Carter, 1995, 46" x 49½"

In my earlier work, grasses represent flexibility and positive change. The introduction of flexible grasses in my support series complements and balances the strength of the backbone.

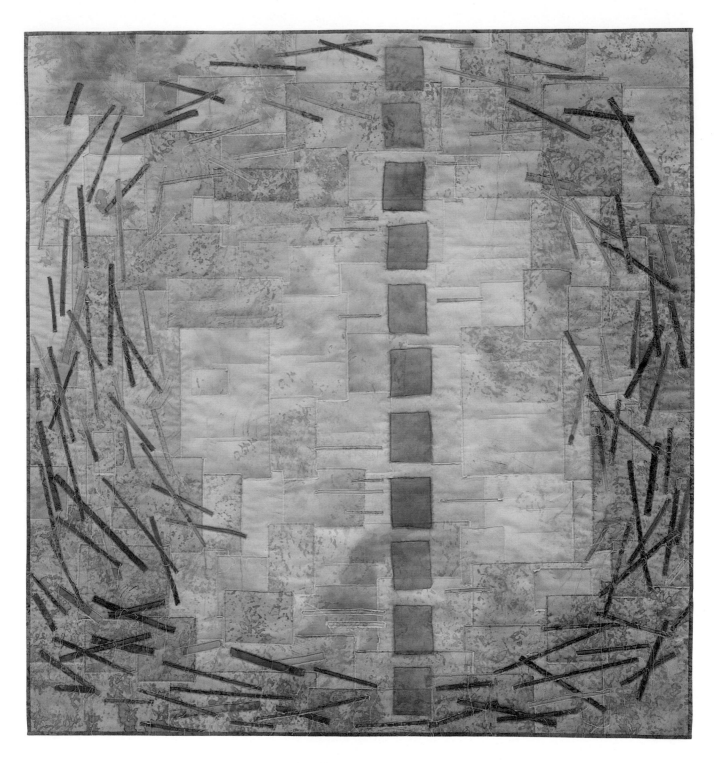

SUPPORT VIII
©Erika Carter, 1995, 46" x 49"

The backbone is surrounded by nest imagery, reflecting the contentment and comfort I find in my new studio space.

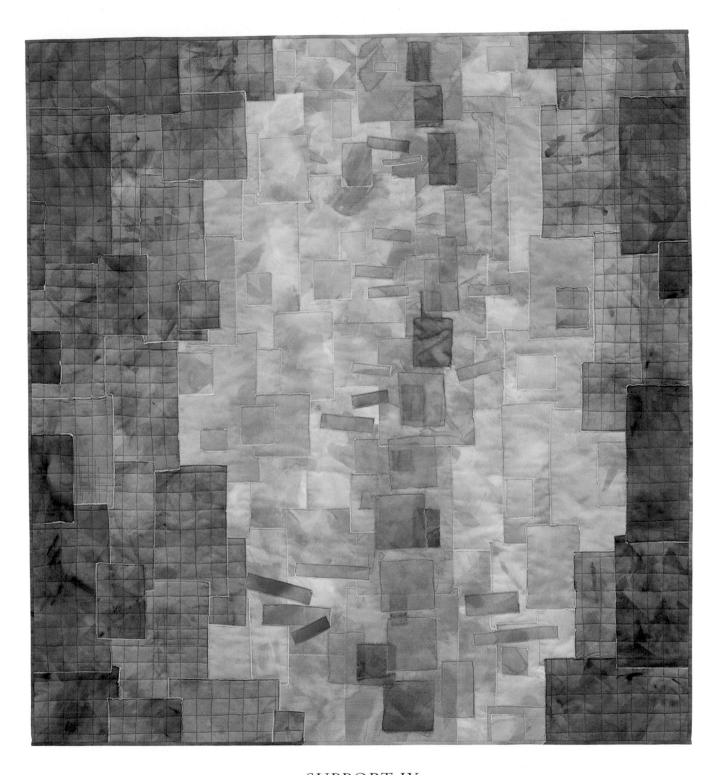

SUPPORT IX
©Erika Carter, 1995, 46" x 49½"

Noted in the character curves of the backbone is the music of stress and support. Each of us emerges from under the jungle-black blanket of mystery ... and dances. (Collection of Mr. and Mrs. R. Fred Hester.)

BIOGRAPHY

Publications

1995

American Craft LV, no. 2 (April/May): 64.

FiberArts Design Book Five. Asheville, North Carolina: Lark Books.

Quilting International XL (March): 38.

Quilt National: Contemporary Designs in Fabric. Asheville, North Carolina: Lark Books.

Quilts: A Living Tradition. Robert Shaw, Hugh Lauter Levin Associates, Inc.

1994

Art/Quilt Magazine I (Premier Issue): 24.

Great Quilting Techniques. Newton, Connecticut: The Taunton Press.

Quilter's Newsletter Magazine, Number 266 (October): 49.

Quilting Today XLIII (August): 66.

Quilting Today XLIV (October): 10–11.

Visions—Quilts, Layers of Excellence. Lafayette, California: C&T Publishing.

1993

American Quilter IX, no. 2, "Taking Chances" (Summer): 19–23.

American Quilter IX, no. 4, "In the Landscape Print Tradition" (Winter): 43.

Contemporary Pictorial Quilts. Wendy Lavitt, Layton, Utah: Gibbs Smith.

Flying Needle, "Life and Art: An Artist's Viewpoint" (November): 5–7.

The New Quilt II. Newton, Connecticut: The Taunton Press.

1992

Award Winning Quilts and Their Makers Vol. II. Paducah, Kentucky: American Quilter's Society.

Quilter's Newsletter Magazine, Number 239 (January/February): 8.

Threads XL (April/May): 39–43.

1991

Aret Runt (Stockholm, Sweden), November: 86–87.

Fiberarts Design Book Four. Ashville, North Carolina: Lark Books.

Great American Quilts 1992. Birmingham, Alabama: Oxmoor House.

The New Quilt I. Newton, Connecticut: The Taunton Press.

Quilter's Newsletter Magazine, Number 232 (May): 8.

Surface Design Journal XV, no. 2: p.18.

The Wall Street Journal, "Quilt Art: Breaking Out of the Bedroom," (July 3).

World of Crafts: Quilting. Laurie Swim, New York, New York: Mallard Press.

1990

The Definitive Contemporary American Quilt. Bernice Steinbaum Gallery, New York, New York.

Fabric Gardens. Cultural Project Department, The Asahi Shimbun (Osaka, Japan).

Landscapes and Illusions. Joen Wolfrom, Lafayette, California: C&T Publishing.

Pacific Northwest XXIV, no. 10 (October): 65.

Quilter's Newsletter Magazine, Number 222 (May): 8.

Visions—Quilts of a New Decade. Lafayette, California: C&T Publishing.

1989

American Quilter V, no. 3 (Fall): 41.

Quilter's Newsletter Magazine, Number 215 (September): 46–47.

1988

Pacific Northwest XXII, no. 3 (March): 31.

1987

The Fiberarts Design Book III. Asheville, North Carolina: Lark Books.

Washington IV, no. 3 (November): 67.

Selected Public and Private Collections

The American Craft Museum, New York, New York

AB Ljusdalshem, Stockholm, Sweden

Kirkland City Hall, Kirkland, Washington

Museum of the American Quilter's Society, Paducah, Kentucky

Omnitrade AB, Stockholm, Sweden

Swedish Hospital, Seattle, Washington

Washington Natural Gas, Seattle, Washington

Weyerhaeuser Real Estate Company, Tacoma, Washington

Nancy Brakensiek, Los Angeles, California

Hilary Fletcher, Athens, Ohio

Sally Reeve, Bellevue, Washington

Sharon Evans Yenter, Seattle, Washington

Exhibition List

1995

Celebrate Art Quilts: Oregon and Washington, The Garret Gallery, Lancaster, Ohio

Contemporary Northwest Quilts, Holter Museum of Art, Helena, Montana

Nonstop Northwest, American Museum of Quilts and Textiles, San Jose, California

Northwest Art Quilts, Bellevue Art Museum, Bellevue, Washington

Northwest International Art Competition, Allied Arts of Whatcom County, Whatcom Museum, Bellingham, Washington

Quilt National '95, The Dairy Barn, Athens, Ohio (Award of Merit, Traveling Exhibition)

Quilts by Members of Studio Art Quilt Associates, Museum of the American Quilter's Society, Paducah, Kentucky

Quilts: Cutting Edges, Jacobs Gallery, Hult Center, Eugene, Oregon

Soft Cuts, Bellevue Community College, Bellevue, Washington

Studio Art Quilt Associates, Maud Kerns Art Center, Eugene, Oregon

1994

American Quilter's Society Tenth Annual Quilt Show, Paducah, Kentucky

Artist As Quiltmaker VI, Firelands Association for the Visual Arts, Oberlin, Ohio

Artist Trust Sixth Annual Art Auction, Seattle, Washington

Erika Carter, Parameters, The American Art Company, Tacoma, Washington (Solo Exhibition)

Fiber Arts Show, North Seattle Community College Art Gallery, Seattle, Washington

Great Pacific Northwest Quilt Show, Seattle Center, Seattle, Washington

Materials: Hard and Soft, Center for the Visual Arts, Denton, Texas

New Work: Makers, Methods, Meaning, Washington State Convention and Trade Center, Seattle, Washington

Northwest Designer Craftsmen Show, Janet Huston Gallery, La Conner, Washington

Pacific Northwest Needle Arts Guild 1994 Annual Juried Fiber Show, Frye Art Museum, Seattle, Washington (Best of Show Award)

Portals, Doorways, Openings, Allied Arts, Richland, Washington

Quilts: Piecing It All Together, Whatcom Museum, Bellingham, Washington

Visions: Quilts, Layers of Excellence, Museum of San Diego History, California

Washington Quilt Artists in Washington, D.C., Senator Patty Murray's Office, Washington, D.C.

World of Quilts XV, John F. Kennedy High School, Somers, New York

1993

Artsplash '93, Redmond Senior Center, Redmond, Washington

Award Winning Quilts, Marymoor Museum, Redmond, Washington

Chesapeake Quilt Festival, Towson, Maryland (Award)

Contemporary Pictorial Quilts Exhibition, Kimball Arts Center, Layton, Utah

Crafts America—The Northwest, Renwick Museum Shop, Washington, D.C.

Erika Carter, Art Quilts, The American Art Company, Tacoma, Washington

Erika Carter, Exterior Wall Gallery, Bellevue Art Museum, Bellevue, Washington

Invitational '93, The Columbus Cultural Arts Center, Columbus, Ohio

Kansas Fiber Directions '93, The Wichita Center for the Arts, Wichita, Kansas (Best of Show Award)

Keep the Pot Hot, Teahouse Kuan Yin, Seattle, Washington

Northwest Designer Craftsmen Exhibit, Bellevue Community College Gallery, Bellevue, Washington

Northwest Designer Craftsmen Show, Art Center Gallery, Seattle Pacific University, Seattle, Washington

Quilt National '93, The Dairy Barn, Athens, Ohio (Traveling Exhibition)

Quilts: Covering the Earth, Birmingham Area Seniors Coordinating Council and Center, Birmingham, Michigan

Textile, Clay, and Metal, Arts West, Seattle, Washington

Textiles, Metal, and Wood, King County Arts Commission Gallery, Seattle, Washington

The Art Pillow: Removing the Tag Under Penalty of Law, Kirkland Art Center, Kirkland, Washington

1992

American Quilter's Society Eighth Annual Show, Paducah, Kentucky

Artsplash '92, Redmond Senior Center, Redmond, Washington (Juror's Award)

Artist as Quiltmaker V, Firelands Association for the Visual
   Arts, Oberlin, Ohio
Bellevue Art Museum Pacific Northwest Annual, Bellevue,
   Washington
Fiberarts Competition and Exhibition, Creative Arts Guild,
   Dalton, Georgia
Kansas Fiber Directions '92, The Wichita Center for the Arts,
   Wichita, Kansas (Award)
*Mercer Island Visual Arts League Twenty-Fifth Summer Arts
   Festival,* Mercer Island, Washington (Second Place)
Needle Expressions '92, Arizona State University Art Museum,
   Tempe, Arizona (Traveling Exhibition)
Northwest Designer Craftsmen Show, Allied Arts Council,
   Richland, Washington
Northwest Designer Craftsmen Show, Arts Council Gallery,
   Everett, Washington
Northwest Designer Craftsmen Show, Ellensburg Art Gallery,
   Ellensburg, Washington
Pacific Northwest Needle Arts Guild 1992 Annual Juried Fiber Show,
   Frye Art Museum, Seattle, Washington (Juror's Choice
   Award)
Quilters' Heritage Celebration, Lancaster, Pennsylvania (Juror's
   Choice Award, First Place)
Quilts: Out of the Mainstream, Red River Revel Arts Festival,
   Shreveport, Louisiana
Tenth Annual Asheville Quilt Competition and Exhibit, Asheville,
   North Carolina (First Place, Judges Choice)
Voices, Tacoma Little Theater, Tacoma, Washington

1991
By Design: The Quilt as Art, Twentieth Northwest Folklife
   Festival, Seattle, Washington
Erika Carter: Modern American Art Quilts, Galleri Bennetter,
   Stockholm, Sweden (Solo Exhibition)
Fourteen Hands: The Quilt As Art, Corvallis Arts Center,
   Corvallis, Oregon
Fragments, 1001 Fourth Avenue Plaza, Seattle, Washington
*Pacific Northwest Needle Arts Guild 1991 Needle Arts and Fiber
   Show,* Peter Kirk Gallery, Kirkland, Washington
Patterns of Identity, University of Washington, Bothell,
   Washington (Award)
Quilt National '91, The Dairy Barn, Athens, Ohio (Traveling
   Exhibition)
Second Northwest Contemporary Quilt Invitational, American Art
   Company, Tacoma, Washington

1990
Artist as Quiltmaker IV, Firelands Association for the Visual
   Arts, Oberlin, Ohio
Contemporary Quilt Association Show, New Pieces Gallery,
   Berkeley, California
The Definitive American Contemporary Quilt, Bernice Steinbaum
   Gallery, New York, New York (Traveling Exhibition)
Erika Carter: Contemporary Art Quilts, American Art Company,
   Tacoma, Washington
Fabric Gardens, Osaka, Japan (Bronze Award, Traveling
   Exhibition to Japan and United States)
Flight of Imagination: Quilts as Art, The Artworks, Ephrata,
   Pennsylvania
Northwest Contemporary Fiber, Paris Gibson Square, Great Falls,
   Montana
Northwest Designer Craftsmen Group Show, Bellevue Art
   Museum, Bellevue, Washington
Northwest Designer Craftsmen Show, Allied Arts Association,
   Richland, Washington
*Pacific Northwest Needle Arts Guild Fifteenth Annual Juried Fiber
   Show,* Frye Art Museum, Seattle, Washington (Juror's
   Choice Award)
Visions—A New Decade, Museum of San Diego History, San
   Diego, California
Visual Arts Show, Forty-Fourth Pacific Northwest Arts and
   Crafts Fair, Bellevue, Washington
Visual Textures, Cunningham Gallery, University of
   Washington, Seattle, Washington (Solo Exhibition)

1989
American Quilter's Society Fifth Annual Show, Paducah, Kentucky
   (Second Place)
Block Party Quilters Show, Bellevue, Washington (Artist in
   Residence)
Breaking New Ground, New England Quilt Museum, Lowell,
   Massachusetts
Crafts 23 Exhibition, Zoller Gallery, Pennsylvania State
   University, Erie, Pennsylvania.
Currents '89, Middle Tennessee State University,
   Murfreesboro, Tennessee
Edmonds Arts Festival, Edmonds, Washington
Galex 23, Galesburg Civic Art Center, Galesburg, Illinois
*Mercer Island Visual Arts League Twenty-Second Summer Arts
   Festival,* Mercer Island, Washington (Second Place)
Northwest Contemporary Quilts, The American Art Company,
   Tacoma, Washington

Northwest International Art Competition, Whatcom Museum of
History and Art, Bellingham, Washington

Paper/Fiber XII, The Arts Center, Iowa City, Iowa

The Personal Icon, Arrowmont School of Arts and Crafts,
Gatlinburg, Tennessee

Piece by Piece: Contemporary Quilts, Foster/White Gallery,
Seattle, Washington

Quilters Heritage Celebration, Sheraton Lancaster Resort,
Lancaster, Pennsylvania (Honorable Mention)

Quilts=Art=Quilts, Schweinfurth Memorial Art Center,
Auburn, New York (Second Place)

Silver Dollar City's Seventh Annual Quilt Show, Branson, Missouri
(First Place)

Visual Arts Show, Forty-Third Pacific Northwest Arts and
Crafts Fair, Bellevue, Washington

Washington Crafts: Then and Now, Tacoma Art Museum,
Tacoma, Washington

West Coast Quilt Show, Gallery Mack, Seattle, Washington

1988

About Fiber, Rockford Art Museum, Rockford, Illinois

American Quilter's Society Fourth Annual Show, Paducah,
Kentucky

Art's Alive! '88, La Conner, Washington

Block Party Quilters Fourth Quilt Show, Redmond, Washington

Contemporary Quilt Association, A Contemporary Theater,
Seattle, Washington

Edmonds Thirty-First Annual Arts Festival, Edmonds,
Washington

Kansas Fiber Directions '88, Wichita Art Museum, Wichita,
Kansas

The Manipulated Thread, Paxson Gallery, University of
Montana, Missoula, Montana

Mercer Island Visual Arts League Twenty-First Summer Arts Festival,
Mercer Island, Washington

*National Standards Council of American Embroiderers' Needle
Expressions '88* (Traveling Exhibition)

Northwest Crafts '88, Tacoma Art Museum, Tacoma,
Washington.

*Pacific Northwest Needle Arts Guild Thirteenth Annual Juried Fiber
Show* 1988, Frye Art Museum, Seattle, Washington
(Juror's Choice Award)

Paper/Fiber XI, The Arts Center, Iowa City, Iowa

Quilts=Art=Quilts, Schweinfurth Memorial Art Center,
Auburn, New York (Juror's Award—Use of Color)

Raintree Quilters Guild Quilt Show, Evansville, Indiana

Silver Dollar City's Sixth Annual Quilt Show, Branson, Missouri

Visual Arts Show, Forty-Second Pacific Northwest Arts and
Crafts Fair, Bellevue, Washington

West Coast Quilters Conference Invitational Quilt Exhibition,
Yakima, Washington

The Wichita National 1988, Wichita Art Association, Inc.,
Wichita, Kansas (Second Place; Jack Lenor Larsen,
Juror)

1987

American Quilter's Society Third Annual Show, Paducah,
Kentucky

Art's Alive! '87, La Conner, Washington

Award Winning Quilts, Marymoor Museum, Redmond,
Washington

Contemporary Quilt Association Show, Edmonds Art Festival
Museum, Edmonds, Washington

Fibers and Form, Bumbershoot, Seattle, Washington

Kansas Fiber Directions '87, Wichita Art Museum, Wichita,
Kansas (Juror's Choice Award)

Quilts=Art=Quilts, Schweinfurth Memorial Art Center,
Auburn, New York

Silver Dollar City's Fifth Annual Quilt Show, Branson, Missouri
(Second Place)

Visual Arts Show, Forty-First Pacific Northwest Arts and
Crafts Fair, Bellevue, Washington

Wearable Art and Fiber Art Show, Kirkland Creative Arts
Center, Kirkland, Washington

1986

Block Party Quilters Third Annual Quilt Show, Bellevue,
Washington (First Place—Most Original)

Edmonds First Annual Quilt Show, Edmonds, Washington (First
Place)

RELATED TITLES FROM
FIBER STUDIO PRESS AND THAT PATCHWORK PLACE

FIBER STUDIO PRESS

Erika Carter: Personal Imagery in Art Quilts
  • Erika Carter
The Nature of Design
  • Joan Colvin
*Velda Newman: A Painter's Approach to
  Quilt Design*
  • Velda Newman with Christine Barnes

Appliqué in Bloom • Gabrielle Swain
Bargello Quilts • Marge Edie
Blockbender Quilts • Margaret J. Miller
Botanical Wreaths • Laura M. Reinstatler
Colourwash Quilts • Deirdre Amsden
Designing Quilts • Suzanne Hammond
Freedom in Design • Mia Rozmyn
Quilted Sea Tapestries • Ginny Eckley
Quilts from Nature • Joan Colvin
Watercolor Impressions
  • Pat Magaret & Donna Slusser
Watercolor Quilts • Pat Magaret & Donna Slusser

Many titles are available at your local quilt shop or
where fine books are sold. For more information,
send $2 for a color catalog to That Patchwork Place, Inc.,
PO Box 118, Bothell, WA 98041-0118 USA.

U.S. and Canada, call **1-800-426-3126** for the name and
location of the quilt shop nearest you.
Int'l: 1-206-483-3313 **Fax:** 1-206-486-7596
E-mail: info@patchwork.com
Web: http://patchwork.com